JOHN MUIR
Wrestles a Waterfall

JULIE DANNEBERG ❧ Illustrated by JAMIE HOGAN

Charlesbridge

In memory of National Park family
vacations!—J. D.

To Peter, Phil, and Marty: Muir
models and wild dads all.—J. H.

Text copyright © 2015 by Julie Danneberg
Illustrations copyright © 2015 by Jamie Hogan

Published by Charlesbridge
85 Main Street, Watertown, MA 02472
(617) 926-0329 ❧ www.charlesbridge.com

Library of Congress Cataloging-in-Publication Data
Danneberg, Julie, 1958–
    John Muir wrestles a waterfall / Julie Danneberg;
Illustrated by Jamie Hogan.
        pages cm
    ISBN 978-1-58089-586-6 (reinforced for library use)
    ISBN 978-1-60734-764-4 (ebook)
    ISBN 978-1-60734-713-2 (ebook pdf)
1. Muir, John, 1838–1914—Juvenile literature. 2. Naturalists—
United States—Juvenile literature. 3. Yosemite Valley
(Calif.)—Juvenile literature. 4. Waterfalls—Juvenile literature.
I. Hogan, Jamie, illustrator. II. Title.
F868.Y6D37 2015
333.72092—dc23 [B]   2013049026

Printed in China
(hc) 10 9 8 7 6 5 4 3 2 1

Illustrations done in Prismacolor and pastel pencil on Canson
    Mi-Teintes paper
Display type and text type set in P22 Stickley Text
Color separations by KHL Chroma Graphics, Singapore
Printed and bound by C & C Offset Printing Co. Ltd.
    in Shenzhen, Guangdong, China
Production supervision by Brian G. Walker
Designed by Whitney Leader-Picone

July 1868

It is by far the grandest of all the special temples of Nature I was ever permitted to enter.

From the sawmill on the creek, John Muir has
a perfect view of the springtime waterfall

CASCADING,

CRASHING,

CAREENING wildly over the side of the mountain.

IN THE SUMMER OF 1868, John Muir left San Francisco looking for "anywhere that's wild." He knew he'd found it when he entered the Yosemite Valley. He was immediately struck by Yosemite's grand beauty and stayed there for ten days. He returned the next fall and stayed until 1871, building and running a small lumber mill.

During the day the sun paints rainbows on the mist that dances around the water's edges. At night, when the stars shine and the bright moon dangles above the valley, moonbows burst from the glowing arc of water as it crashes into the evening shadows. For John, the sight and sound of the waterfall is one of the pleasures of living in Yosemite Valley.

When Muir first came to Yosemite Valley, he lived in a small cabin he built himself, where he slept in a hammock hung over an indoor spring "entering in one end and flowing out the other." Later on he lived at the sawmill. He kept his journals, sketches, and books in a room he called "the hang-nest" because it jutted out from the side of the mill like a balcony. He slept in the sawmill itself and could see the stars and Yosemite Falls through windows in the roof.

Sometimes John isn't content to observe the waterfall's magnificence from the comfort of his cabin. Sometimes its beauty lures him outside for a closer view.

RALPH WALDO EMERSON, the famous American writer, visited Yosemite in 1871 and met Muir. Emerson was so impressed with him that he invited Muir to travel east for an extended visit. Muir declined, not wanting to leave his newly discovered paradise. Almost twenty years later he finally visited Emerson's hometown, Concord, Massachusetts.

And so, one night in early April, John stands in the
shadow of the mountain and looks at and listens to the
waterfall. But on this night, admiring its beauty from
below isn't enough. John wants to be closer still.

MUIR DIDN'T just love nature, he studied it. He rambled through the woods and mountains and often brought plant specimens home with him. His friends loaned him science and geology textbooks, which he used to teach himself about nature and the world around him.

He climbs up, over loose and slippery gravel beds. Up through dark woods. Up beside the thundering vertical river until he reaches Fern Ledge. He is so close to the waterfall that the mist brushes his face, the noise pounds in his chest, and the night feels alive with the energy of the twisting, misting, roaring water. For a moment John is perfectly content. But then he wants to be closer still.

AN INTREPID MOUNTAINEER, Muir thought nothing of setting off on a two-day, fifty-mile hike with nothing but a loaf of bread in his pocket. He forged rugged paths through heavy brush, crossed rushing streams, scrambled across boulder fields, and scaled rocky mountainsides.

John spies a granite ledge that cuts across the rock wall. He eases out onto the narrow precipice, flattening himself against the dripping, slippery granite. Inch by inch he moves toward the waterfall until he can reach out his hand and touch the frigid, rushing water.

And he is happy.

THROUGHOUT HIS LIFE Muir recorded
thoughts, adventures, scientific observations,
and drawings of plants and mountains in
his journal, which he carried, along with a
magnifying glass, attached to his belt. He
was a prolific writer, and the material for
his published writing often came directly
from his journals.

Suddenly, a strong breeze lifts the heavy curtain of water away from the hard granite wall. Quickly, John scoots behind the

TUMBLING,

RUMBLING,

TWISTING,

MISTING,

FOAMING,

THUNDERING waterfall.

FOR MUIR, nature provided joy. He loved the beauty of a single snowflake, the music of the wind during a windstorm, the smell of pines, and the touch of the sun on his face. He felt that nature wasn't something to be feared, but enjoyed and appreciated.

Now John is as close as he can be. He peeks out at the moon through the moving veil of water. The music of the falls surrounds him. This is glorious! John's heart soars, pounding out his excitement in rhythm with the falling water.

MUIR ALWAYS TRIED to experience nature up close. He slept on a rock in the middle of a river. He climbed a one-hundred-foot Douglas fir tree during a storm. He stood outside in the midst of an earthquake. He had no limits when it came to experiencing nature firsthand.

Then the wind stops.
SWISH!
The heavy curtain of water drops back into place.
SMASH!
John is pinned against the jagged granite wall.
BANG!
Water pounds onto John's head and shoulders,
threatening to sweep him off the narrow ledge
and into the thundering column of water.

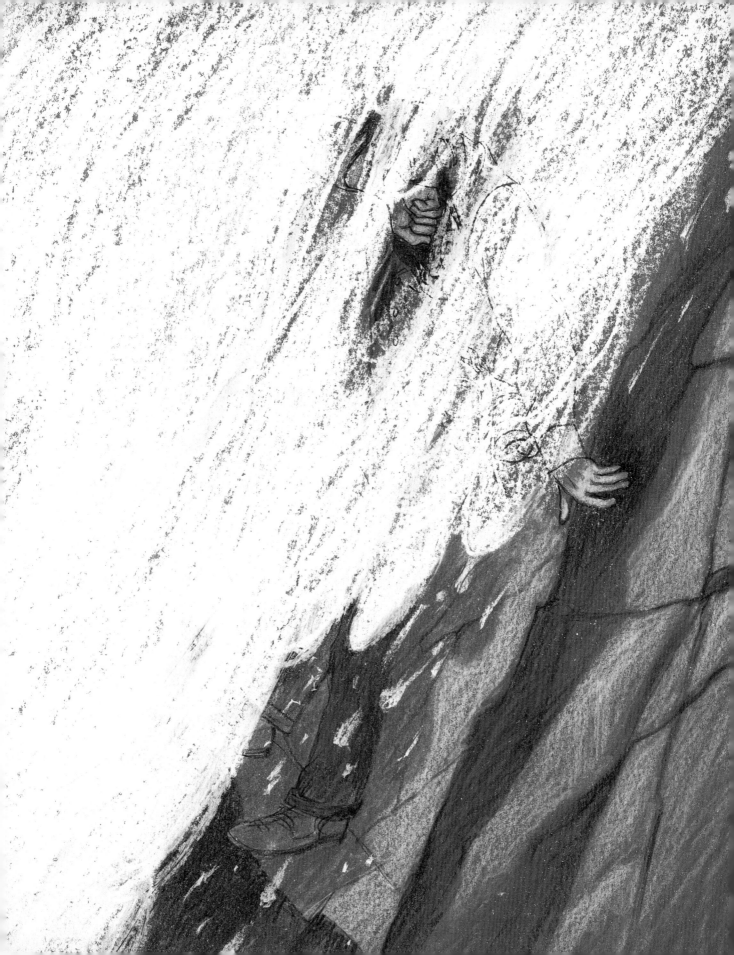

Now the space behind the waterfall isn't so glorious. It is dark. And cold. And dangerous. Now the thundering in John's chest comes from fear. He tries to protect his body from the pounding torrents of water.

And he WAITS.

And SHIVERS.

And WAITS.

And SHAKES.

And WAITS some more.

Luckily the fickle wind shifts and lifts the curtain of water, just a bit. The pounding lessens, just a bit. John can move, just a bit. And he does. He slowly and carefully makes his way out from behind the beautiful, dangerous, magical, scary waterfall. Inch by inch John creeps back toward the safety of the trail.

Shivering with cold and relief, John returns to the comfort and warmth of the hang-nest. He climbs into bed and is soon lulled to sleep by the thundering noise of the water as it crashes into the river below.

April 1871

Two evenings ago, I climbed the mountain to the foot of the upper Yosemite Falls....My wetting was received in a way that I scarcely care to tell. The adventure nearly cost all.

JOHN MUIR'S YOSEMITE

By the time he'd lived in the Yosemite Valley for five years, John Muir was well known for his knowledge of science and nature, his skill as a mountain guide, and his ability to spin a good story. He put these skills to excellent use as a writer. On December 5, 1871, an article he wrote about the glaciers in Yosemite was published by the *New York Tribune*. Then on New Year's Day, 1872, the same newspaper printed another of John's pieces, entitled "In the Yo-semite: Holidays Among the Rocks." (The title was later changed to "Yosemite in Winter.") Muir realized that a writer's life would allow him to earn a living and still give him the freedom to continue his scientific explorations. For many years Muir lived and wrote in the San Francisco Bay Area in the winter and spent the rest of the year in Yosemite. Readers loved the stories of his adventures and his detailed descriptions of nature's beauty. In fact, the *Century Illustrated Monthly Magazine* published two versions of Muir's essay about the April 3, 1871, waterfall adventure portrayed in this book, first in 1890 and again in 1912. Muir described at the end of the 1890 essay how he felt about the incident:

> *Somewhat nerve-shaken, drenched, and benumbed, I . . . reached my cabin before daylight, got an hour or two of sleep, and awoke sane and comfortable, better, not worse, for my wild bath in moonlit spray.*

Muir's passion for nature also fueled his desire to preserve it. He used his skills as a writer to support nature preservation, and many people responded, including President Theodore Roosevelt, who visited him in Yosemite in 1903. They went camping together, and Muir talked about the importance of preserving America's wilderness. Partially as a result of that camping trip, Roosevelt created national parks and monuments, and he set aside millions of acres of conservation land in the United States during his presidency. Later in life John Muir founded the Sierra Club, which is still one of the most important nature-conservation organizations in the US. His passion for nature continued throughout his life.

The trail that John Muir climbed to get to Fern Ledge, halfway up Yosemite Falls, is still there. But it's not maintained and is dangerous, so very few of the park's visitors use it. Newer trails to hike up Yosemite Falls or to view the falls from below are available to the more than one million annual visitors to the park. The waterfall has a 2,425-foot drop—equal to a 240-story building. (That's almost as tall as two Empire State Buildings stacked on top of each other!) It is a temporal waterfall, which means it exists only during certain times of the year. Since the water that creates the waterfall comes from Yosemite Creek, fed by melting snow from the Sierra Nevada, the falls usually begin running in early April and dry up later in the summer.

1838–1914

LEARN MORE

John Muir's essay about his waterfall experience can be found online by searching for its title: "A Perilous Exploration of the Yosemite Fall."

Explore the life and legacy of John Muir through the Sierra Club's online John Muir Exhibit, featuring photographs, a biography, and access to many of his published works.
www.sierraclub.org/john_muir_exhibit/

Find John Muir's personal papers online through the University of the Pacific.
www.pacific.edu/Academics/Schools-and-Colleges/College-of-the-Pacific/About/Centers-and-Institutes/John-Muir-Center.html

The National Park Service's website about Yosemite and John Muir offers rich history and information.
www.nps.gov/yose/historyculture/muir.htm

Episode two of Yosemite National Park's *Yosemite Nature Notes* video series focuses on Yosemite Falls. It provides a firsthand view of and lessons about the falls' incredible power and beauty. Search for the video on the Internet.

Muir Woods National Monument, near San Francisco, offers hikes, tours, and information about redwood tree conservation and John Muir's life and work.
www.nps.gov/muwo/index.htm

BOOKS ABOUT JOHN MUIR

Ehrlich, Gretel. *John Muir: Nature's Visionary.* Washington, DC: National Geographic, 2000.

❀Lasky, Kathryn. *John Muir: America's First Environmentalist.* Cambridge, MA: Candlewick, 2006.

❀Locker, Thomas. *John Muir: America's Naturalist.* Golden, CO: Fulcrum, 2003.

Melham, Tom. *John Muir's Wild America.* Washington, DC: National Geographic, 1976.

❀Rosenstock, Barb. *The Camping Trip That Changed America.* New York: Dial Books for Young Readers, 2012.

Stetson, Lee. *The Wild Muir: Twenty-two of John Muir's Greatest Adventures.* San Francisco: Yosemite Conservancy, 2013.

❀Wadsworth, Ginger. *John Muir, Wilderness Protector.* Minneapolis: Lerner, 1992.

White, Fred. *Essential Muir: A Selection of John Muir's Best Writings.* Berkeley, CA: Heyday, 2006.

Wilkins, Thurman. *John Muir: Apostle of Nature.* Norman: University of Oklahoma Press, 1995.

Worster, Donald. *A Passion for Nature: The Life of John Muir.* New York: Oxford University Press, 2008.

❀books for kids

CITATIONS

"It is by far the grandest...". Muir, letter to Mrs. Carr, July 16, 1868.
http://digitalcollections.pacific.edu/cdm/ref/collection/muirletters/id/18367

"anywhere that's wild": Wilkins, p. 57.

"entering in one end . . .": Muir, unfinished memoirs.
http://www.sierraclub.org/john_muir_exhibit/life/life_and_letters/chapter_7.aspx

"Two evenings ago . . ." and "the hang-nest": Muir, letter to his sister Sarah Galloway, April 5, 1871.
http://digitalcollections.pacific.edu/cdm/ref/collection/muirletters/id/19122